W9-BAC-577

ARGENTINA

ABDO
Publishing Company

ARGENTINA

by Erika Wittekind

Content Consultant
Andrés Avellaneda
Professor Emeritus, University of Florida

CREDITS

Published by ABDO Publishing Company, 8000 West 78th Street, Edina, Minnesota 55439. Copyright © 2012 by Abdo Consulting Group, Inc. International copyrights reserved in all countries. No part of this book may be reproduced in any form without written permission from the publisher. The Essential Library™ is a trademark and logo of ABDO Publishing Company.

Printed in the United States of America,
North Mankato, Minnesota
062011
092011

 THIS BOOK CONTAINS AT LEAST 10% RECYCLED MATERIALS.

Editor: Melissa York
Copy Editor: Susan M. Freese
Series design and cover production: Emily Love
Interior production: Kazuko Collins

About the Author: Erika Wittekind is a freelance writer and editor living in Wisconsin. She has a bachelor of arts degree in journalism and political science from Bradley University. She has covered education and government for several community newspapers, winning an award for best local news story from the Minnesota Newspapers Association for 2002. She focused her career on children's nonfiction in 2008.

Library of Congress Cataloging-in-Publication Data
Wittekind, Erika, 1980-
  Argentina / by Erika Wittekind.
    p. cm. -- (Countries of the world)
  Includes bibliographical references and index.
  ISBN 978-1-61783-105-8
  1. Argentina--Juvenile literature. I. Title.
  F2808.2.W58 2011
  982--dc23
                                    2011018525

Cover: Mount Fitzroy, Patagonian Andes, Argentina

TABLE OF CONTENTS

CHAPTER 1
A VISIT TO ARGENTINA

Your plane touches down at the Ezeiza International Airport in Buenos Aires, Argentina. Drowsy from the ten-hour flight from the United States, you wonder what you will find in the southernmost country in South America. Will you have a chance to learn how to tango? Will you have a run-in with a large cat—maybe a jaguar or a puma? Once outside, a warm breeze hits your face, and you find it hard to believe you are in the country whose southern tip practically brushes Antarctica. Then again, you are also just a few hundred miles south of a subtropical rain forest.

Your journey around Argentina may take you north to the Brazilian border to see the Iguazú Falls, two-thirds of which are within Argentina. This magnificent collection of 275 waterfalls makes Niagara Falls look

Aerial view of Buenos Aires, capital of Argentina

EVITA

When many people think of Argentina, they think of *Evita*, the Andrew Lloyd Webber musical based on the life of Eva Perón. A film version of the musical, starring Madonna and Antonio Banderas, came out in 1996. Both dramas follow the life of Eva Perón from a child of the lower class to an influential political wife to her early death from cancer. The government of Argentina also made a 1984 documentary titled *Evita: Quien Quiera Oír Que Oiga (Evita: Who Wants to Listen May Hear)*. The movie was meant to counter the historical inaccuracies allegedly contained in the Lloyd Webber version.

like your kitchen sink in comparison. On the subantarctic end of this very long country, you might walk among penguins or see an ice chunk the size of a bus fall from a glacier into the sea. In between, you will want to visit the Andes, your guidebook tells you, to gaze at the Western Hemisphere's highest peak, Mount Aconcagua.

But first, you hop aboard a shuttle heading northeast into the heart of Buenos Aires, which approximately one-third of the country's population calls home. At first, it looks like any big city—Victorian houses, tall skyscrapers, neighborhood restaurants—and you feel strangely at home. But as your journey continues, you start to notice how alive, how colorful this vibrant city is—from the rainbow-colored, pressed-tin houses of the La Boca neighborhood to the brightly colored murals that adorn storefronts

The Iguazú Falls are on the border of Brazil and Argentina.

LAND OF TANGO

Milongas, or tango salons, can be found throughout the capital. Performances and dance events take place every night of the week. Most newcomers enjoy taking in the spectacle from the sidelines, but tourists who want to learn this passionate dance can arrive early, when many of the milongas offer lessons.

and subway tunnels. Any night of the week, you can find people dancing the tango, which originated in Argentina.

Known as the "Paris of the South" and the "birthplace of tango," Buenos Aires, the nation's capital, is heavily shaped by its European roots and by its multinational population.[1] It is divided into a number of barrios, or neighborhoods, each with its own distinctive international flavor. Buenos Aires has its own Chinatown, as well as neighborhoods settled by immigrants from elsewhere in South America. In the highly cultured Recoleta, known for its fashionable boutiques, French architecture, and fine hotels, tourists and wealthy Argentines enjoy outdoor street performances, art exhibits, and craft fairs. To experience old-world Buenos Aires, you will want to visit San Telmo—a barrio so historic that the entire neighborhood is designated as a National Historic Monument. There, cobblestone streets are lined with tall trees and public lanterns, called *faroles,* that create a romantic atmosphere after dark.

Dancers tango in the streets of Buenos Aires.

OVERCOMING THE PAST

As you dance, shop, look at art, and dine on fine cuts of steak, you may come to think that the *porteños*—as residents of Buenos Aires are known—have it all. But first impressions can be misleading. Underneath the colorful neighborhoods, passionate dancing, and European glamour, Argentina is still reeling from a deeply troubled past. This is a country that a century ago was poised to become an economic power that would rival China, France, or the United Kingdom. From abundant natural resources to an educated and cultured people, Argentina seemed to have all the elements needed to emerge as a prosperous economy. Instead, it plummeted toward third-world status and has struggled to achieve its potential.

For much of the twentieth century, Argentines suffered under brutal military dictatorships.

FROM PROSPERITY TO POVERTY

In 1930, Argentina was the seventh-richest country in the world, but by 1980, it had fallen to seventy-seventh on that list.[2] By 2010, Argentina had rebounded somewhat, attaining the twenty-fourth highest gross domestic product (GDP) in the world.[3] Peter Calvert, a political scientist specializing in Latin American studies, wrote about the country's unrealized promise: "'Argentina,' people said, 'is the land of the future, always has been and always will be.'"[4]

A *farole* will light this street in the La Boca neighborhood after dark.

Whenever a democratically elected leader took power, any decision disapproved of by the military would result in his or her removal in a swift military coup. Power changed hands frequently and often by force. Those decades were marked by violence, as political parties clashed and dissent was quashed. In 2006, Argentines marked the thirtieth anniversary of the Dirty War—a time when the military government arrested, tortured, and killed tens of thousands of innocent citizens.

Argentina comes from the Latin word for silver, *argentum.*

Amid political struggles and human rights abuses, Argentina lost its economic footing. Disastrous and inconsistent policies led to spiraling inflation and widespread poverty. In the early 1980s, Argentina started to overcome its violent past as a series of democratically elected leaders enacted policies that stabilized the economy. The country suffered another setback in 2001, when a severe recession led to riots and political turmoil. But unlike in the turbulent times of the past, democracy prevailed, and Argentina continued on the road to stabilization.

POLITICALLY CHARGED ATMOSPHERE

The country's checkered past is never far from the minds of Argentines. This is why, in addition to its European sophistication, Buenos Aires is

Over the years, the Plaza de Mayo in Buenos Aires has been the site of many political protests.

BOLIVIA

PARAGUAY

Tropic of Capricorn

JUJUY
Jujuy ⊙
SALTA
Salta ⊙
FORMOSA
Formosa ⊙
Asunción ⊛
TUCUMÁN
CHACO
MISIONES
Tucumán ⊙
SANTIAGO DEL ESTERO
Resistencia ⊙
CATAMARCA
Catamarca ⊙
Santiago del Estero ⊙
Corrientes ⊙
Posadas ⊙
La Rioja ⊙
CORRIENTES
BRAZIL
LA RIOJA
SANTA FE
SAN JUAN
CÓRDOBA
Santa Fe ⊙
San Juan ⊙
Córdoba ⊙
Paraná ⊙
Mendoza ⊙
ENTRE RÍOS
Santiago ⊛
Rosario •
URUGUAY
San Luis ⊙
SAN LUIS
Buenos Aires ⊛
MENDOZA
La Plata ⊙
Montevideo ⊛
Río de la Plata
Santa Rosa ⊙
BUENOS AIRES
ARGENTINA
CHILE
LA PAMPA
Bahía Blanca ⊙
Mar del Plata •
NEUQUÉN
Neuquén ⊙
RÍO NEGRO
Viedma ⊙
PACIFIC OCEAN
San Carlos de Bariloche ⊙
San Matías Gulf
Chubut
Rawson ⊙
CHUBUT
ATLANTIC OCEAN
San Jorge Gulf
SANTA CRUZ
Bahía Grande
Río Gallegos ⊙
Strait of Magellan
FALKLAND ISLANDS
(UNITED KINGDOM)
TIERRA DEL FUEGO
Ushuaia ⊙

NORTH
↑

Legend:
— International boundary
— Provincial boundary
⊛ National capital
⊙ Provincial capital
• City or village

0   200 Miles
0   200 Kilometers

Political Boundaries of Argentina

known for its politically charged atmosphere. While democracy has succeeded for several decades, concerns persist about government corruption and human rights abuses.

Stay in the Argentine capital long enough, and you might witness a political demonstration in front of the presidential palace in the Plaza de Mayo in downtown Buenos Aires. Historically, this beautiful building has been a favorite site for protesters and political demonstrations.

POLITICS IN THE AIR

Danny Palmerlee, author of a guidebook on Argentina, wrote about the current atmosphere: "Travelers who dig beneath the tourist-office version of Argentina will find a cultural climate electrified by discussion, argument and creative fervor. Argentina is in the throes of reinvention, and many people have a lot at stake. . . . Spend any amount of time here, and you'll find yourself wrapped up in the discussion too, hopefully with a couple of locals. Argentines are, after all, some of the most amicable, seductive, engaging folks on the planet."[5]

The tradition dates back to 1945, when supporters of Juan Perón converged outside the palace to protest his imprisonment. The Mothers of the Plaza de Mayo—an organization formed by women in 1977 to protest the abduction of their children during the Dirty War—still gathers there every Thursday to raise awareness of social issues. Finally confident that gross human rights abuses are safely in Argentina's past, they no longer refer to these meetings as protests.

CHAPTER 2

GEOGRAPHY: RAIN FORESTS AND GLACIERS

Spanning 2,360 miles (3,800 km) from north to south, Argentina encompasses a wide range of climates and terrains.[1] Whereas the northernmost area is characterized by wondrous waterfalls and subtropical rain forests, in the south, monstrous glaciers are still carving their path through Patagonia. Between these extremes are temperate forests and fertile plains. And linking the two vastly different climates are the towering Andes, which line the entire western length of the country. With such geologic and climatic diversity, it can be said that this southernmost country in South America just about has it all.

Covering a little more than 1 million square miles (2.7 million sq km), Argentina is approximately three-tenths the size of the United States.

The Perito Moreno Glacier in Santa Cruz in southern Patagonia

ARGENTINE ANTARCTICA

Argentina claims approximately 374,519 square miles (970,000 sq km) of Antarctica as its national territory, although sections of this land overlap territory claimed by the United Kingdom and Chile.[4] Argentine explorers first visited the continent in 1881. Argentina operates four scientific bases on Antarctica.

This makes Argentina the eighth-largest country in the world and the second-largest nation in South America.[2] To the north and northeast, Argentina shares borders with Bolivia, Paraguay, Brazil, and Uruguay. To the west, it shares its longest border with the long and narrow country of Chile, and to the south and southeast, it meets the South Atlantic Ocean.

Argentina is divided into 23 provinces and one federal district, Buenos Aires, which has been the capital since 1776. Approximately one-third of the population lives in Gran Buenos Aires, which includes the city and surrounding suburbs. As of 2009, Gran Buenos Aires had a population of approximately 12.3 million people.[3]

REGIONS OF ARGENTINA

Argentina has four major regions: the North, the Andes, the Pampas, and Patagonia. The North is made up of three subregions, the Andean Northwest, Mesopotamia, and the Chaco. Chaco, in the northeast, is a relatively flat, subtropical region with lush forests and land that has been

BOLIVIA
PARAGUAY
Tropic of Capricorn

Legend:
- International boundary
- ⊛ National capital
- • City

0   200 Miles
0   200 Kilometers

Pilcomayo
Bermejo
•Salta
Asunción ⊛
Iguazú Falls
•Tucumán
Salado
•Corrientes
Paraná
BRAZIL

Andes Mountains

Mount Aconcagua
30°   30°
Santa Fe•
Córdoba•
•Mendoza
Uruguay
Santiago ⊛
Rosario•
Salado
URUGUAY
Buenos Aires ▪
Montevideo ⊛
La Plata•
Río de la Plata
Pampas
•Victorica
Cape San Antonio
Santa Rosa•
ARGENTINA
CHILE
•Bahía Blanca
•Mar del Plata
Colorado
•Neuquén
Negro
40°   40°
•Viedma

PACIFIC
OCEAN

San Matías Gulf
Valdés Peninsula
Chubut
•Rawson
Chico
Punta Tombo
ATLANTIC
OCEAN
•Sarmiento
San Jorge Gulf
Patagonia
Deseado
Cape Tres Puntas
Chico
50°   50°
Bahía Grande
Río Gallegos
Cape Vírgenes
FALKLAND ISLANDS
(UNITED KINGDOM)
Strait of Magellan
Laguna del Carbon

Legend:
- Cropland
- Pasture
- Forest
- Mountain region
- Barren land

Tierra del Fuego
•Ushuaia
Isla de los Estados
NORTH
↑
Cape Horn
80°   70°   60°   50°

Geography of Argentina

IGUAZÚ FALLS

One of the most popular tourist sites in Argentina is Iguazú Falls, which consists of more than 275 waterfalls that cascade down from heights of up to 269 feet (82 m).[5] About two-thirds of Iguazú Falls is in Argentina, and one-third is in Brazil. The word *Iguazú* translates to "great waters" in the native Guaraní language. The falls can be seen via a lower path that leads to the base or an upper path that features a footbridge.

cleared for agriculture. Mesopotamia is the name given to the fertile valley between the Uruguay and Paraná Rivers. In addition to the popular tourist destination of Iguazú Falls, Mesopotamia features plains, hills, and jungles with an abundance of wildlife. The dry, mountainous Andean North is known for its mining and energy resources. It contains large oil and natural gas reserves.

Central Argentina, which is known as the Pampas, is a large expanse of flat and very fertile land. Approximately 400 miles (640 km) wide, it extends from Buenos Aires to the eastern foothills of the Andes. The weather is temperate, with more rainfall in the south Pampas than in the north. Considered to be the heartland of Argentina, the Pampas contains not only the national capital but also the majority of agricultural and industrial production for the country.

Grassland in the Pampas

AVERAGE TEMPERATURES AND RAINFALL

Region (City)	Average January Temperature Minimum/ Maximum	Average July Temperature Minimum/Maximum	Average Rainfall January/July
East Central/Pampas (Victorica)	59/93°F (15/34°C)	37/59°F (3/15°C)	2.8/0.6 inches (7.1/1.5 cm)
Buenos Aires (Buenos Aires)	63/84°F (17/29°C)	43/57°F (6/14°C)	3.1/2.2 inches (7.9/5.6 cm)
Northeastern Interior (Corrientes)	72/95°F (22/35°C)	54/73°F (12/23°C)	5.5/2.2 inches (14/5.6 cm)
Western/Cuyo (Mendoza)	61/90°F (16/32°C)	36/59°F (2/15°C)	0.9/0.2 inches (2.3/0.5 cm)
Southern/Patagonia (Sarmiento)	52/79°F (11/26°C)	28/45°F (–2/7°C)	0.2/0.6 inches (0.5/1.5 cm)
Extreme South (Ushuaia)	45/57°F (7/14°C)	30/39°F (–1/4°C)	1.5/1.1 inches (3.8/2.8 cm)[6]

The southernmost region of Argentina, Patagonia, is also the largest. The plateau is dry, windy, and cool, with bitter cold in the southernmost portions. It is sparsely populated and home to industries including oil, gas, aluminum, and fisheries, as well as a significant ecotourism industry. In the south, more than 300 glaciers make up the Patagonian Ice Field. They include the Perito Moreno Glacier, which is 3 miles (4.8 km) wide and 200 feet (60 m) tall and covers 100 square miles (260 sq km).[7]

The central Andes region, edged by a narrow strip of desertlike landscape, is known as Cuyo. This region includes some of the highest peaks in the Andes, including Mount

LAND OF FIRE

Located at the southern tip of South America, Tierra del Fuego is an archipelago consisting of a large island, Isla Grande, and several smaller islands. It is separated from the mainland by the Strait of Magellan. The western half of Isla Grande is owned by Chile, while the eastern half is the Argentine province of Tierra del Fuego. The Argentine half is home to Ushuaia, the southernmost city in the world. Ushuaia is used as a launch point for expeditions to Antarctica.

Tierra del Fuego gets its name from the lifestyle of the indigenous inhabitants who lived there before being conquered by Europeans. This southern area of Argentina was home to the Selk'nam, Haush, Yaghan, and Alacaluf peoples, who were hunters and gatherers. They wore little clothing but stayed close to constant fires to stay warm—even in their canoes. For this reason, the Spaniards gave the area the name Tierra del Fuego, which means "Land of Fire."

EXTREMES

Argentina is home to both the lowest and highest points in the Western Hemisphere. Mount Aconcagua, located in the Argentine Andes, is the Western Hemisphere's tallest mountain. Located in the northwestern corner of the Mendoza province, this peak reaches 22,835 feet (6,960 m) above sea level. Laguna del Carbon stakes its claim as the lowest point in the Western and the Southern hemispheres, at 344 feet (105 m) below sea level.[8] It is located in Great San Julián's Depression, a salt lake area in the Santa Cruz province in southeastern Argentina.

Aconcagua. The region is also famous for its wine production and large ranches.

CLIMATE

Because Argentina is located in the Southern Hemisphere, the seasons are reversed from those in North America. Summer lasts from December to February, and winter occurs in June, July, and August. Most of the country is temperate in climate, except in the areas farthest north and south.

Located just south of the Tropic of Capricorn, the northern part of Argentina has a subtropical climate. In the subtropical forests and eastern Chaco, high temperatures and rainfall occur all year. Western Chaco is similar, except that the first half of the year is fairly dry. The northern

Mount Aconcagua is the tallest mountain in the Americas.

CHAPTER 3

ANIMALS AND NATURE: FROM PENGUINS TO PUMAS

On the remote Punta Tombo peninsula of Patagonia, ecotourists and scientists flock to see the hundreds of thousands of Magellanic penguins that gather there each September to breed. A few decades ago, their numbers were estimated at 1 million on this narrow strip of land jutting approximately 2 miles (3.2 km) into the Atlantic Ocean. But oil released from ships coats their feathers and kills them. Increased fishing has cut their food supply. Now, the colony numbers approximately 400,000 penguins per year.[1]

Eric Wagner, a journalist writing for *Smithsonian* magazine online, recounted the spectacle he witnessed while surrounded by thousands of penguins one September evening:

Magellanic penguins in Patagonia

I watch as one dives underwater, flicks its wings and glides towards the shore, a swift shadow in a breaking wave. It pulls up with a neat, tight turn and hops onto the beach, where its feet promptly become entangled in a piece of kelp, and it falls on its face. Somewhat resignedly (or so it seems to me), it rights itself, shakes off and starts a slow, metronomic trudge up to the berm, joining hundreds of other penguins on their way to nests that may be more than half a mile inland. These birds have not set foot on land in almost six months, and it shows.[2]

SAVING THE PENGUINS

Scientist Dee Boersma has studied the Magellanic penguins of Punta Tombo for more than 25 years. She estimated that from the 1980s to the early 1990s, oil accounted for the deaths of approximately 40,000 penguins per year.[3] Through tracking, she found that the birds' migration paths to Brazil and Uruguay closely match the routes taken by ships.

Boersma discovered that the oil leaked or discarded by these ships actually created a worse pollution problem in the ocean than occasional large oil spills. When the penguins encounter oil slicks, the substance damages their feathers' ability to insulate their bodies, and they die from the cold. Widespread public protests pushed the government to alter shipping routes. After that, the number of penguins falling victim to oil declined dramatically.

Penguins are not the only animals worth seeing in Patagonia. The dry Punta Tombo peninsula is also home to guanacos, a relative of the llama, armadillos, skunks, and scorpions. Sea lions, elephant seals, whales, and orcas can also be seen off the Atlantic coast.

WILDLIFE OF ARGENTINA

As a large country with many varying climates and geographic features, Argentina is home to a wide array of plant and animal life. As a whole, the country has approximately 360 mammals, 1,000 bird species, 700 different fish, 400 reptiles and amphibians, and 20,000 plant species.[4] The puma, also known as a cougar or mountain lion, is considered by many to be the unofficial national animal. Pumas can be found in Patagonia and northern Argentina. The national bird is the hornero, which is small and brown with a long beak. The red flower of the ceibo tree is the national flower.

The puma has the largest range of any North American land animal—from Alaska to Argentina.

Away from the coast, Patagonia is covered in small shrubs and other plants that can withstand the arid climate. Coniferous forests cover areas in the far west. Pumas, wild horses, miniature deer called pudú, wild boar, armadillos, and a large rodent called a mara also roam the mountainous region.

Northeast Argentina features some of the most exotic plant and animal species, from the capybara, the world's largest rodent; to the caiman, which is a relative of the crocodile; to the black howler monkey. Large, colorful birds fill the trees and the skies. Historically, jaguars were prominent in north and central Argentina, but they are now declining in numbers.

The Andean condor and the California condor are two distinct species.

The central Pampas, which are covered in tall grasses, are home to animals including armadillos, Pampas cats, and birds such as hawks, herons, and falcons. In dry northwest Argentina, cacti are one of the few plants to thrive. Animals of the Northwest include llama and guanaco. Flamingos and other migratory birds can be spotted near the region's salt lakes. The dry Cuyo features thorny shrubs and plants that survive with little water. The largest flying bird in the Americas, the condor, soars in the Andes.

The hair of the guanaco can be spun into soft yarn.

DEFORESTATION AND ENDANGERED SPECIES

Similar to other industrialized countries, Argentina faces concerns about deforestation. According to the World Wildlife Fund, Argentina had 259 million acres (105 million ha) of forests in 1914. Recent studies show that number has declined to between 69 and 111 million acres (28 and 45 million ha).[5] In particular, expansion of soybean agriculture has led to deforestation in the Chaco. Beef production has threatened grasslands and forests in central Argentina. In Patagonia, sheep and cattle grazing have damaged the ecosystem.

The International Union for the Conservation of Nature categorized 16 species of animals in Argentina as critically endangered and 49 as endangered.[6] Critically endangered species include the short-tailed chinchilla,

MONKEY PUZZLE TREES

One of Argentina's most distinctive trees is the monkey puzzle tree, a conifer native to southern Argentina. The tree earned its name after a colonist remarked about the difficulty a monkey would have climbing it (although no monkeys live in its habitat). The tree's pointed, triangular leaves last up to 15 years and can pierce like a needle. The tough bark of the tree makes it highly fire resistant, and it can live more than 1,000 years. The oldest known monkey puzzle tree is more than 800 years old.

Ranches have changed the original habitat of Patagonia.

ENDANGERED SPECIES IN ARGENTINA

According to the International Union for Conservation of Nature (IUCN), Argentina is home to the following numbers of species that are categorized by the organization as critically endangered, endangered, or vulnerable:

Mammals	37
Birds	50
Reptiles	5
Amphibians	29
Fishes	36
Mollusks	0
Other Invertebrates	12
Plants	44
Total	213[7]

a rodent that may be recovering due to hunting and trapping laws; the candelabra tree, a casualty of deforestation; and the glaucous macaw, a large, blue bird that was targeted by hunters and may now be extinct. Among the endangered species are the sei, blue, and fin whales, which can sometimes be viewed off the Atlantic coast; Andean cats, which live high in the mountains; and river otters, which have lost much of their habitat to fisheries.

POLLUTION AND CLIMATE CHANGE

Pollution in Argentina stems largely from the country's cattle and soybean industries, as well as from waste dumps and automobiles. However, Argentina has made itself a leader in setting emissions limits. In 1998, President Carlos Menem committed to strict targets for the reduction of greenhouse gases. Argentina was the first developing country to do so and one of the first nations to set precise limits.

Amid concerns about climate change, scientists have kept a close eye on the ice fields of Patagonia. The Perito Moreno Glacier has maintained its size for the past century, growing as the snow melts in the Andes and retracting as it sheds ice chunks into the lake below. But Upsala Glacier, which used to be one of the largest glaciers in South America, is shrinking at a rate of 46 feet (14 m) per year.[8] Other glaciers also appear to be receding. The consequences of shrinking glaciers may include a declining water supply for area residents and farms, rising sea levels that could threaten coastal cities, and unpredictable weather patterns.

PREHISTORIC GIANTS

Remains of the largest dinosaur known to science were discovered in the Patagonia region of Argentina in 1987. *Argentinosaurus huinculensis*, an herbivore, measured 131 feet (40 m) long and 59 feet (18 m) high. Its long neck stretched three to four stories into the sky. The largest carnivorous dinosaur, the *Giganotosaurus*, was also discovered in Patagonia. It measured 45 feet (14 m) long. These dinosaurs were alive 85 to 95 million years ago during the Cretaceous period, when what is now the Patagonian desert was a lush landscape.[9]

Scientists disagree about whether the changes are due to climate change or to other factors related to the natural environment. In 2010, Argentina passed a law to protect its glaciers. The law includes a plan to inventory the country's glaciers every five years and prohibits disposal of contaminants in the glacial environment.

NATIONAL PARKS

To preserve its vast array of wildlife, Argentina has designated 28 national parks along with a number of nature and educational reserves.[10] The purpose of the national parks is to encourage biodiversity, to preserve the environments of endangered species, to maintain the sites of paleontological discoveries, and to promote education and scientific research.

Hikers negotiate wet patches atop Perito Moreno Glacier. Argentina is worried about its shrinking glaciers.

CHAPTER 4

HISTORY: FROM COLONY TO REPUBLIC

Historians believe humans first arrived in North America approximately 50,000 years ago by crossing a land bridge between Asia and Alaska. Slowly moving south, the migrants reached the vicinity of modern-day Argentina by approximately 13,000 BCE. The ancient inhabitants of this area were a mixture of nomadic hunters and gatherers and primitive farmers who lived in small, unrelated groups representing many different cultures and languages. Because these groups were so decentralized, it took several centuries for the Europeans to take control of the Southern Cone. Instead of conquering one empire, they faced resistance from many individual groups.

Patagonia's early inhabitants left paintings and hand tracings such as this one in caves.

successful Spanish settlements in modern-day Peru, Bolivia, Chile, and Paraguay. In some places, such as Córdoba, the Spaniards encountered violent resistance from the native tribes. Disorganized and hampered by inferior weapons, the indigenous peoples could not fight off the Spanish. Buenos Aires was reestablished in 1580 when Juan de Garay led a group of Spaniards and mestizos, descendents of the Europeans and the Guaraní, to settle in the city.

Spain dictated that all of its trade with the colonies had to go through Lima in Peru. With no authorized trade routes, Buenos Aires became home to smugglers. In the late eighteenth century, Spain shifted its trade through Buenos Aires, and the city quickly grew to be the population center of Argentina.

INDEPENDENCE FROM SPAIN

By the end of the eighteenth century, Argentine-born colonists, or creoles, were anxious to be free of Spain's rule. In 1806 and 1807, the British twice tried to take control of Buenos Aires, causing high-ranking Spaniards to flee. The creoles never let the Spanish officers return to their previous positions of power.

Buenos Aires declared independence from Spain on May 25, 1810. Led by General José de San Martín, the provinces that would later

This monument in Buenos Aires commemorates early colonizer Juan de Garay.

CAUDILLO-STYLE POLITICS

Historian Jonathan C. Brown, author of *A Brief History of Argentina*, explains how nineteenth-century political unrest set a tone for Argentine politics that continued into modern times: "Nineteenth-century caudillo-style politics became identified with unstable political leadership, assassinations, coups and countercoups, civil unrest, intimidation of critics, and the flouting of the constitution. It has endured and is practiced even today. Most Argentine citizens can recount numerous instances of caudillo-style politics during the last quarter of the twentieth century."[1]

comprise the Argentine Republic declared their independence from Spain on July 9, 1816. Similar declarations were being made throughout South America, and Spanish rule was mostly banished from the continent by the 1820s.

The lack of Spanish authority set off regional conflicts for much of the rest of the nineteenth century. Residents of Buenos Aires wanted power to be centralized there. Residents of other provinces, who resented Buenos Aires for its unshared wealth and European influence, supported a federalist system that would share power between the national government and the provinces and maintain the provinces' autonomy. The 1820s were marked by numerous conflicts between the provincial leaders, called caudillos, and civil unrest. In 1835, federalist Juan Manuel de Rosas became dictator and preserved the caudillos's power over their provinces. But Rosas left a violent legacy, including the creation of the *mazorca* a ruthless governmental police force, and the use of torture and terror tactics. He was removed from office in 1852.

CREATION OF THE ARGENTINE REPUBLIC

In 1853, the Argentine Republic was founded with the creation of a national constitution, which was approved by a convention in Santa Fe on May 1. Justo José de Urquiza, who had overthrown Rosas, became the country's first president. In 1862, Buenos Aires became the official capital.

The constitution established a strong central government and granted the president power to intervene in provincial matters in times of political turmoil. However, the nation was not yet fully united. Provinces still maintained their own military forces. Between 1865 and 1870, Argentina allied with Uruguay and Brazil against Paraguay in a border-dispute war known as the War of the Triple Alliance. The need to mobilize forces for the war helped unify the provinces.

Justo José de Urquiza led Argentina from 1852 to 1860.

For the next half a century, Buenos Aires, and to a lesser extent the other provinces, enjoyed a period of economic prosperity. European investment and immigration, as well as improving infrastructure, combined to boost the economy. Industries such as beef, grain, and wool were thriving. Two new classes emerged—one consisting of professionals, such as lawyers and bankers, and the other of urban immigrant workers.

Juan and Eva Perón, 1950

THE RISE OF JUAN PERÓN

Even during this brief golden age, racial discrimination and class divisions bubbled beneath the surface of Argentine society. In 1912, secret ballots were introduced to combat electoral corruption, and Argentina elected its first president through popular vote. Power transitions were relatively peaceful until a band of military personnel overthrew the government in 1930 during a period of economic decline and social unrest.

In the years that followed, which became known as the Infamous Decade, a group of mostly conservative politicians stayed in power because they were backed by the armed forces. Tensions grew over the use of force and fraud to keep the group in power, and the rise of an

EVA PERÓN

Eva María Duarte was born to a poor family in 1919. At 15, she moved to Buenos Aires and became a radio performer and actress. She met Colonel Juan Perón during fund-raising efforts for an earthquake. When he was imprisoned in 1945, she helped organize a demonstration to get him released, and they were married a few days later. During her husband's presidency, Eva was an outspoken leader of women Peronistas. She worked on behalf of underprivileged Argentines and was active in promoting women's suffrage.

Eva Perón ran the María Eva Duarte De Perón Welfare Foundation to assist the poor with clothing, housing, food, and health care. She also assisted the Ministry of Health in its efforts to fight diseases and to build new hospitals. She often interacted with the poor on a personal level, and her warmth and dedication to charity made her a revered figure in Argentina. Eva Perón died of cervical cancer in 1952 at age 33.

attempt in 1982 to seize custody of the Falkland Islands from the United Kingdom.

DEMOCRACY TAKES HOLD

President Raúl Alfonsín was elected in 1983 and set out to restore democracy, to reduce the military's power, and to put on trial high-ranking perpetrators of the Dirty War. Controversy over who would be prosecuted or pardoned continued for more than a decade. Because of the military's ongoing influence, relatively few officials from the era ended up being punished at this time.

MOTHERS OF THE PLAZA DE MAYO

Out of fear, most Argentines remained quiet about the people who disappeared during the Dirty War. In April 1977, a group of female relatives of those that had disappeared started to gather in silent protest at the Plaza de Mayo in Buenos Aires every Thursday. Attention from the foreign media and governments, such as Sweden, Spain, and France, is thought to have protected these women from being punished by their own government.

Alfonsín grew unpopular because of his unsuccessful attempts to curb soaring inflation, which in 1985 was estimated at 1,129 percent annually.[5] Peronist Carlos Menem was democratically elected in 1989. Not since 1928 had power passed from one democratically elected leader to another without military intervention.

The Mothers of the Plaza de Mayo protest the loss of their loved ones, 1979.

In the 1990s, Menem's economic policies finally brought inflation under control. President Fernando de la Rúa was elected in 1999. However, a new economic crisis struck in 2001. As the entire economy

Weathering several crises, the Argentine National
Congress continues to operate normally.

seemed about to collapse, the country experienced a run on the banks, high unemployment, and public protests that resulted in thousands of arrests. On December 20, 2001, President de la Rúa fled, and four different interim presidents took power over the course of two weeks. Riots and a crime wave wreaked havoc, and descendents of immigrants moved back to their families' home countries.

A few decades earlier, this kind of crisis might have led to a military coup in Argentina. But this time, constitutional processes were followed, and the nation emerged with its democracy intact.

Carlos Menem was jailed twice for political reasons before later becoming president.

CHAPTER 5

PEOPLE:
A CHANGING NATION

The Argentine people of today are radically different from the population just two centuries ago. When Argentina declared its independence from Spain in 1816, it had a population of less than 500,000. More than 100,000 of these people were mestizos compared to just 10,000 of European descent.[1] Massive immigration by Europeans, combined with the systematic elimination of native tribes, combined to reverse this situation.

By July 2010, Argentina had a population of more than 41 million. Ninety-seven percent of the population was white; these people are mostly of Spanish and Italian descent. Mestizos, Indians, and other nonwhite groups accounted for a mere 3 percent combined.[2]

At the turn of the twentieth century, almost half of the immigrants were Italian.

Argentine people celebrated their cultural heritage at an international folk festival in Buenos Aires, July 17, 2010.

HISTORIC PEOPLES

Early inhabitants of Argentina became known as Indians after European explorers mistook the Americas for the country of India. In the sixteenth century, approximately 300,000 Indians, belonging to many separate tribes, resided in what is now Argentina.[3] These included farmers, such as the Guaraní, and bands of hunters, such as the Araucanians.

After the Spanish arrived, Spanish colonists and their descendents, called creoles, became the country's elite class.

GAUCHO CULTURE

From the seventeenth to the late nineteenth centuries, gauchos—similar to the cowboys of North America—roamed the Pampas on horseback. As mestizos, they treasured their freedom and untamed lifestyle. Wild horses became their steeds, and they captured and killed wild or escaped livestock for food.

Gauchos were recognizable by their distinctive appearance: typically, a brightly colored shirt, baggy trousers with a wide leather belt decorated with coins or pieces of silver, boots, and a straw hat. Gauchos often had long hair and a thick beard. A gaucho commonly used his horse's sheepskin saddle as a bed.

As civilization took over the Pampas, the gaucho lifestyle largely disappeared. However, the gaucho tradition lives on in Argentine literature and art.

Gauchos—Argentine cowboys—were often mestizos.

YOU SAY IT!

English	Spanish
Hello	Hola (OH-lah)
Good-bye	Adiós (ah-DYOHS) or Ciao (CHOW)
Good morning	Buenos días (BWEH-nahs DEE-ahs)
Good evening	Buenas noches (BWEH-nahs NOH-chehs)
Please	Por favor (POHR fah-BOHR)
Thank you	Gracias (GRAH-syahs)
You're welcome	De nada (DEH NAH-dah)

Paraguay, Aymara near Bolivia, and Mapuche in parts of Patagonia. Some Argentines also learn to speak English, Italian, French, or German.

Ninety-two percent of Argentines are Roman Catholic, 2 percent are Protestant, and 2 percent are Jewish.[6] The vast majority of Argentines subscribe to Roman Catholicism, yet only one in five actively practices the Catholic faith. According to the official Web site of the Argentine government, 2,500 cults and religions are officially recognized.[7]

Although citizens are guaranteed freedom of religion, the Argentine constitution gives special consideration to the Catholic church.

POPULATIONS OF MAJOR CITIES

Buenos Aires: 2,970,950

Córdoba: 1,267,774

La Plata: 600,000

Mar del Plata: 600,000

Mendoza: 130,000

Rosario: 908,163

Tucumán: 527,607

San Carlos de Bariloche: 274,509[11]

12.3 million people lived in Gran Buenos Aires, which includes the city and surrounding suburbs.[10] Outside the Buenos Aires area, there are only a handful of significant population centers, such as Córdoba, Mendoza, Rosario, and La Plata.

The lights of Buenos Aires brighten the night.

CHAPTER 6

CULTURE: THE LAND OF THE TANGO

Argentina's most significant cultural contribution, as well as a great source of national pride, is likely the style of dance and music called the tango. In the late nineteenth century, traditional dances such as waltzes, polkas, and mazurkas were popular among all social classes. The tango is thought to have evolved out of local interpretations of dances such as the polka and mazurka by adding more exaggerated movements and intricate flourishes. It quickly earned a reputation as the vulgar pastime of criminals and prostitutes, but in reality, it was first enjoyed by members of the lower working class and urban poor. Still, in the lower-class dancing clubs that were popular with gangsters, activities such as drinking, gambling, and prostitution occurred alongside the tango.

In Argentina, guests are expected to arrive at parties 30 to 45 minutes late.

Buenos Aires hosted the 2010 Tango Dance World Festival and Championship.

of La Boca, where brightly colored houses and murals are still common. Among the most famous murals in Argentina are those at the high-class Galerías Pacífico shopping center in Buenos Aires. A group of artists including Antonio Berni, Juan Carlos Castagnino, Manuel Calmiero, Lino Enea Spilimbergo, and Demetrio Urruchúa created the murals when the building was remodeled in 1945. Street art experienced a resurgence in the twenty-first century when graffiti artists started covering buildings with politically charged artwork after the economic and political crisis of 2001.

AN OSCAR WIN

In 2010, the Academy Award for the Best Foreign Language Film went to the Argentine movie *El Secreto de Sus Ojos* (*The Secret in Their Eyes*). It tells the story of a detective trying to solve a 25-year-old rape and murder case that took place during the Dirty War. The win was huge news in Argentina, which is the only Latin American country to ever win an Oscar. Another Argentine movie won an Academy Award in 1985: *La Historia Oficial* (*The Official Story*).

LITERATURE

With high rates of literacy and education, Argentines have long placed a priority on literature. Early Argentine works feature the culture of the gaucho, the Argentine equivalent of a cowboy. More traditional novels became popular in the twentieth century.

Argentine Juan José Campanella directed the Academy Award–winning film *El Secreto de Sus Ojos*.

RICARDO
DARÍN
SOLEDAD
VILLAMIL
PABLO
RAGO
Y LA PARTICIPACIÓN ESPECIAL DE
GUILLERMO
FRANCELLA
UN CRIMEN. UN MISTERIO. UN AMOR.
EL SECRETO DE SUS VIDAS ESTÁ A PUNTO DE ESTALLAR.
EL SECRETO
DE SUS OJOS
UNA PELÍCULA DE JUAN JOSÉ CAMPANELLA
www.elsecretodesusojos.com

versions are less spicy than their counterparts in other countries. In Buenos Aires, restaurants feature a variety of international cuisine. Street vendors sell empanadas, gelato, and sausage sandwiches called *choripans*.

Argentina's many vineyards have earned a reputation for producing good wine. Another traditional drink is yerba maté, a hot tea served in a gourd and drunk through a filtered straw. The consumption of yerba maté is a ritual that is shared among friends, family members, or colleagues.

SPORTS

The most popular sport in Argentina, by far, is soccer. Part of the reason that soccer has become so widespread is that it does not require expensive equipment, so it is easily accessible to everyone. Children start playing soccer at a young age, some of them for several hours per day. Playing, watching, and discussing soccer are a big part of everyday life for many Argentines.

Buenos Aires alone has 24 professional soccer teams. Argentina has been home to several world-class soccer players, including Diego Maradona and Lionel Messi. Considered by many to be the world's greatest soccer player, Maradona led Argentina to win the World Cup in 1986. The Argentine team also won the World Cup in 1978 and the

Argentines eat twice as much beef as Americans.

A traditional Argentine breakfast usually includes yerba maté and croissants.

Olympic gold medal in 2004 and 2008. Argentines also enjoy playing tennis, field hockey, rugby, basketball, and volleyball. Although less popular, a pololike sport called *pato* is the official national sport.

As in many countries, Argentines call soccer "football."

Fans cheer for the Boca Juniors, a Buenos Aires team.

CHAPTER 7
POLITICS: INCREASING STABILITY

During the economic disaster of 2001, unemployment and prices skyrocketed, the peso weakened, and half the population of Argentina descended into poverty.[1] But the military had less power than in previous times of unrest, and Argentines treasured their democracy too much to return to the days of bloodshed. Eduardo Duhalde became the fourth interim president to be appointed by Congress as 2001 came to an end. He took office on January 2, 2002. Duhalde managed to stabilize the peso and to negotiate a deal with the International Monetary Fund to reduce the country's level of debt. But perhaps his greatest achievement in two years was merely to maintain order until the next election.

The sun symbol on the Argentine flag represents the Incan sun god and honors the appearance of the sun from clouds on May 25, 1810, during the first rally for independence.

JUSTICE FOR THE DIRTY WAR

As a leftist Peronist in the 1970s, Néstor Kirchner faced persecution by the military. Once president, he took the opportunity to finally seek justice for the crimes of the Dirty War. First, he fired 75 percent of his army generals and 50 percent of his naval and air force officers to rid the military of Dirty War supporters.[3] Then, he repealed amnesty laws that had prevented officers from being prosecuted. Hundreds faced charges, although only a small number were actually convicted. Additionally, Kirchner apologized on behalf of the government and dedicated a memorial at the former Navy Mechanics School, a site where many of the atrocities occurred.

In 2003, Peronist Néstor Kirchner was elected president. Kirchner became popular for his reversal of policies that protected military leaders of the Dirty War, his disapproval of governmental corruption, and his favorable economic policies. While he provided for the country's stability, Kirchner became a much more powerful leader than is allowed in some other democracies, such as the United States. The Argentine Congress granted Kirchner emergency powers, which he used to issue 249 presidential decrees during his four-year term. By contrast, he sent only 176 bills to be passed by Congress.[2] Congress even granted him the power to fund parts of the budget without congressional approval.

Cristina Fernández de Kirchner served in Congress while her husband was president.

Despite Kirchner's popularity, concerns about corruption have persisted in Argentina. When his term ended after four years, his wife, Cristina Fernández de

**Néstor Kirchner and
Cristina Fernández de Kirchner**

CRISTINA FERNÁNDEZ DE KIRCHNER

In 2007, Cristina Fernández de Kirchner became the first female elected president of Argentina. The widow of former president Néstor Kirchner and a trained lawyer, Fernández served one term in the House of Deputies and was elected to the National Senate three times before running for president. She became known for her strong personality and her work on human rights and women's issues. Similar to other Peronists, Fernández has supported large social welfare programs and welcoming policies toward immigrants. Her popularity has suffered slightly due to the effects of the global recession on Argentina, but she has succeeded on several fronts. For example, in 2010, she introduced a bill that Congress passed to authorize same-sex marriage.

As a prominent woman in Argentine politics, Fernández has been compared to Eva Perón, but she dismisses the likeness. "Eva was a unique phenomenon in Argentine history, so I'm not foolish enough to compare myself with her. Women of my generation owe her a debt: When we came of age during the dark [military] dictatorship of the 1970s, we had her example of passion and combativeness to get us through."[5]

Kirchner, ran for president in 2007. Some people speculated that the couple planned to stay in power by taking turns running for president, but Néstor Kirchner died in 2010. At the time of Fernández's campaign, her husband's defense minister was accused of tax evasion, while the economics minister was found to possess a bag containing a large amount of unexplained cash. Money was also allegedly smuggled in from Venezuela for Fernández's campaign. Because of Kirchner's popularity and an improving economy, however, Fernández easily won the election with 45 percent of the vote.[4]

CONSTITUTION OF THE ARGENTINE NATION

Argentina's original constitution, approved in 1853, established a federal republic with a strong central government that reserved some powers for the provinces. The constitution has remained in place since then, although it has been suspended during military takeovers of the government. The constitution has also been amended or revised several times to change specific items, such as lengths of terms and distribution of seats in the legislature. In 1949, during the presidency of Juan Perón, it was amended to allow him to run for additional terms. Perón also added a list of social rights. The current version of the constitution was adopted in 1994 when Carlos Menem was president.

Adopted in 1813, the Argentine national anthem is 40 years older than the constitution.

In some ways, the Argentine constitution is similar to the US Constitution, on which it was modeled. The current constitution guarantees a free press, fair trials, universal suffrage, and the right to bear arms. While it expresses support for the Roman Catholic religion, it also provides for freedom of religion. Additionally, it ensures rights for workers, such as reasonable working hours, paid vacations, the right to strike, and equal pay for equal work. Some of the rights guaranteed by the constitution are:

To work and perform any lawful industry; to navigate and trade; to petition the authorities; to enter, remain in, travel through, and

*leave the Argentine territory; to publish their ideas through the
press without previous censorship; to make use and dispose of their
property; to associate for useful purposes; to profess freely their
religion; to teach and to learn.*[6]

EXECUTIVE AND LEGISLATIVE BRANCHES

The constitution established Argentina as a federal republic with
three branches of government: executive, legislative, and judicial. In the
executive branch, the
president and vice president
serve four-year terms,
and they may serve up to
two consecutive terms.
The executive branch
is particularly strong
because it has the ability to
introduce legislation and
can exercise the power
of the line-item veto. In
times of extreme turmoil,
the constitution gives the

REQUIREMENTS FOR OFFICE

A candidate for the House of Deputies must be
at least 25 years old and must have been a citizen
for a minimum of four years. A candidate for the
Senate must be at least 30 years of age, must have
been a citizen for at least six years, and must have a
minimum annual income of at least 2,000 Argentine
pesos. In addition to meeting the requirements for
becoming a senator, the president must also be a
natural-born Argentine citizen.

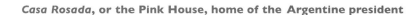

Casa Rosada, or the Pink House, home of the Argentine president

STRUCTURE OF THE GOVERNMENT OF ARGENTINA

Executive Branch	Legislative Branch	Judicial Branch
President Vice president	National Congress Upper House: Senate Lower House: House of Deputies	Supreme Court Lower courts

president additional powers to issue decrees that do not have to be passed by Congress.

The Argentine Congress makes up the legislative branch and has two houses. The lower house of the legislature is the House of Deputies; it has 257 members that are distributed between the provinces based on population. Deputies serve four-year terms, and half the deputies stand for election every two years. The House of Deputies must introduce all bills relating to raising money and recruiting troops, and it has the exclusive power to impeach the president, vice president, or other officials. Since 1991, Argentine law has required that one-third of all

The Argentine Congress meets in the National Congress building in Buenos Aires.

candidates for the lower house from each political party be female. This law has allowed many Argentine women to rise to power.

The Senate is the upper house of Congress and has 72 members, three from each province, who serve six-year terms. Similar to the United States, the vice president serves as president of the Senate and votes only to break a tie. If the House of Deputies votes to impeach a leader, the Senate conducts the impeachment trial.

The Argentine flag was adopted in 1816. The blue bands symbolize the free skies.

JUDICIAL BRANCH

The judicial branch consists of a Supreme Court and lower courts. The Supreme Court had seven judges as of 2011, but in 2006, the National Congress approved a plan to gradually reduce the number of judges sitting on the court to five. A council of magistrates appoints federal judges, and they must then be approved by the Senate. The constitution allows the president to issue pardons for some crimes.

Historically, Argentina has had a weak judicial branch that has been undermined by the legislative and executive branches. For example, in the decades following the Dirty War, laws were passed to place limitations on who could be tried and to put a deadline on prosecutions.

Argentines rally in the Plaza de Mayo

CHAPTER 8

ECONOMY: RECOVERING PROSPERITY

In 1900, Argentina seemed full of promise to become one of the world's economic powers. It was a major exporter of wheat, wool, and beef. By 1913, its per capita income was similar to that of France or Germany, and a strong middle class had emerged. But power rested mostly with a small group of wealthy landowners who shaped policies to benefit themselves while millions of immigrants remained powerless. "Prosperity came almost too quickly to Argentina," writes Douglas Brinkley in a foreword to *Argentina: What Went Wrong*. "Land, demand, and profit created an oligarchy that soon dominated politics as well as wealth."[1]

Due to greed and shortsightedness, Argentina fell behind the rest of the world in industrializing and diversifying its economy. Imports soon exceeded exports, and the government began accumulating a high level

At the beginning of the twentieth century, wealthy landowners controlled Argentina. Today, ranching is still important to the economy.

THE URBAN POOR

In Argentina, the working poor and the unemployed make their presence known by picketing while banging pots and pans, blocking roads, and harassing public officials. They have even seized public buildings and taken over workplaces. *Piqueteros*, or picketers, participate in well-organized demonstrations, give press conferences, and run soup kitchens. Violence has broken out during some demonstrations, causing the police to become involved. Leaders of the piqueteros have tried to run for office and to persuade officials to grant more aid to the poor.

Another group of poor people is known as the *cartoneros*, who scavenge for recyclables that can be turned in for money. They have campaigned for public and police tolerance of their lifestyle. In the words of one cartonero, "Behind each one of us there is a story. We are fathers, mothers of family without formal work, unwed mothers."[2]

of debt. Even in its apparent golden age, Argentina was in an unstable financial position.

When the country began to industrialize in the early twentieth century, workers spent long hours in unsanitary and unsafe conditions. Many lived in slum areas, where the lack of plumbing and piles of garbage made disease a problem. Labor unrest led to hundreds of strikes that disrupted trade, while class divisions sometimes resulted in outbursts of violence. Support grew for Marxism, which rejects

Socialists demonstrate in Argentina in 1939.

capitalism and supports an authoritarian government that would plan the economy.

The damaging effects of World War I and the world economy and the devastating Wall Street crash of 1929 did not spare Argentina. It experienced declining income and rising unemployment, which caused decreased government revenues. The situation resulted in a military coup in 1930, the first in a long series of military interruptions of constitutional presidencies in twentieth-century Argentina.

Today, Argentina has the fifteenth-fastest rate of economic growth in the world.

In the 1940s, President Juan Perón took steps to support labor unions, raise wages, and protect the rights of urban and rural workers. Under Perón's authoritarian regime, the state took control of key industries and utilities. While these changes were underway, innovation, productivity, and profits suffered, triggering gross inflation. "Wages became a political reward rather than an exchange for time and labor," notes Colin M. MacLachlan in *Argentina: What Went Wrong*. "The economy seemed locked in a downward spiral of declining exports, foreign exchange problems, inadequate investments, corruption, smuggling, and capital flight."[3]

After Perón was overthrown, the next decades were shaped by military coups, periods of violence, and failed attempts to curb inflation and improve the economy. In the 1980s, democracy was restored but other problems remained. Inflation soared to more than 1,000 percent, and foreign debt reached $46 billion—an amount the government

seemed to have no hope of repaying.[4] Many newspapers and magazines
went out of business, creating a new setback for democracy.

RECOVERY AND CRISIS

In 1989, President Carlos Menem took office and went to work on the economy. He slashed military spending and social programs, privatized state industries, cracked down on tax evasion, and took steps toward restoring a free market economy. In 1991, the Convertibility Law got rid of the old currency, the austral, and froze the exchange rate between the peso and the US dollar; one Argentine peso would always be equal to one US dollar. Inflation was brought under control, and the economy finally stabilized. Menem also set out to foster good trade relations with the United States and countries in Latin America and Europe.

ROAD TO DEFAULT

Between the 1970s and 1990s, the Argentine government generated a huge level of debt. Investors viewed Argentina as an acceptable risk and had confidence the country would make good on the loans. With money so easy to come by, Argentine politicians did not pay attention to warnings to stop overspending. By 1998, the nation carried a foreign debt equal to 41 percent of its gross domestic product (GDP).[5]

These measures had disastrous consequences, however. Menem's conversion to a free market economy was marred by corruption. While wealthy and politically connected Argentines benefited, many educated Argentines lost their jobs. Unemployment and poverty swelled. Part of the problem was that the peso continued to be linked to the US dollar. When the dollar became worth less in Europe, so did the peso, and Argentina found itself unable to compete for European trade.

The financial crisis peaked in 2001, when President Fernando de la Rúa tried to prevent a run on the banks by limiting people's money withdrawals. The action was followed by rising violence. Following de la Rúa's resignation, an interim president declared a default because the country would not be able to pay its debts. The default on the country's approximately $140 billion foreign debt was the largest in world history.[6]

Eduardo Duhalde took office on January 2, 2002. He unlinked the peso from

Argentine pesos

COMMUNITY SURVIVAL

Many Argentines survived the 2001–2002 economic crisis by bartering for goods and services, selling treasured possessions, and forming neighborhood cooperatives to purchase necessities. Employers that were short of money resorted to paying their employees in goods, which they exchanged for other goods. In some cases, workers took over factories that were about to be shut down and kept them running. The cooperation within communities that was needed for survival also led to increased involvement in civic activities.

the dollar and took other steps to stabilize the economy. A year later, President Néstor Kirchner was elected, and he is largely credited for putting Argentina back on the right path. In 2005, Kirchner negotiated to restructure and repay the country's overwhelming debt, saving billions of dollars. "His role in rescuing Argentina's economy is comparable to that of Franklin D. Roosevelt in the Great Depression of the United States," wrote Mark Weisbrot, codirector of the Center for Economic and Policy Research in Washington DC. "Like Roosevelt, Kirchner had to stand up not only to powerful moneyed interests, but also to most of the economics profession, which was insisting that his policies would lead to disaster."[7]

In 2010, Argentina's debt was approximately half of its GDP.

EMERGING ECONOMY

Since the crisis of 2001–2002, Argentina has been making a slow but sure recovery founded on its reduced debt, revived industry, increased exports, and improved fiscal policies. From 2002 to 2008, the gross domestic product (GDP) grew by an average of 8.5 percent per year.[8] However, the country has faced setbacks during the recent worldwide recession and still struggles to keep inflation under control. In 2010, the officially released inflation rate for consumer goods was 11 percent, although a US government source suggested that the actual rate could be

Shanty town outside Buenos Aires

two to three times more than that.[9] In addition, as of 2005, approximately one-third of all Argentines still lived in poverty, and 12 percent lived in extreme poverty.[10]

UNEMPLOYMENT AND POVERTY

During the economic crisis of 2001–2002, unemployment reached an estimated high of 25 percent, and almost 60 percent of Argentines were living below the poverty line. As the economy has recovered, the unemployment rate has fallen steadily. In 2010, it was officially reported as 7.9 percent. Likewise, the percentage of Argentines living below the poverty line has decreased in recent years. In 2009, the officially reported rate was 12 percent.[14]

Today, Argentina is the third-largest economy in Latin America, after Brazil and Mexico.[11] It is an industrialized nation with a strong agriculture sector and rich natural resources. In 2010, Argentina had the twenty-fourth highest GDP in the world, with a per capita GDP of $14,700.[12] Its main trade partners are Brazil, China, the United States, Germany, and Chile. Argentina is known worldwide for its beef and for its wine, and it is also a major exporter of cereals. Other main exports are petroleum, chemicals, and machinery and transport equipment. Major imports include machinery, cars, oil, natural gas, other chemicals, and plastics.

In the labor force, 72 percent of Argentines work in the service industry, 23 percent work in industry, and 5 percent work in agriculture.[13]

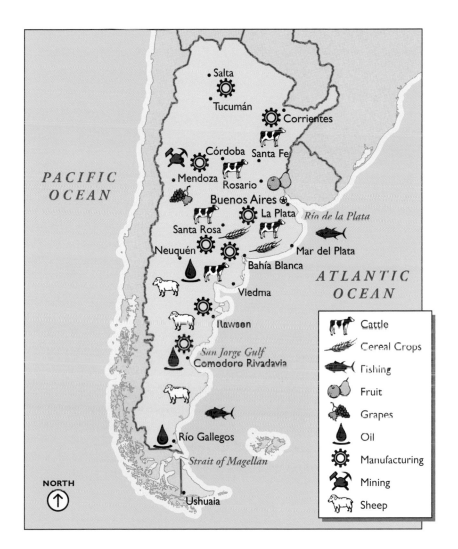

Salta

Tucumán

Corrientes

Córdoba **Santa Fe**

Mendoza **Rosario**

Buenos Aires

La Plata

Río de la Plata

Santa Rosa

Neuquén

Mar del Plata

Bahía Blanca

Viedma

PACIFIC OCEAN

ATLANTIC OCEAN

Rawson

San Jorge Gulf
Comodoro Rivadavia

Río Gallegos

Strait of Magellan

NORTH

Ushuaia

Cattle	
Cereal Crops	
Fishing	
Fruit	
Grapes	
Oil	
Manufacturing	
Mining	
Sheep	

Resources of Argentina

INFRASTRUCTURE

Argentina has more than 1,000 airports—the sixth most of any country in the world. Argentina also has the eighth-largest railway system in the world. Of the nation's roadways, 43,131 miles (69,412 km) are paved, and 100,639 miles (161,962 km) are unpaved.[15] Argentina also benefits from modern communication technology, and telephones, cellular phones, televisions, and the Internet are widely available. Fiber-optic cables are being installed between cities.

The country's chief industries include food processing, printing, and manufacturing cars, consumer durables, textiles, chemicals, and metals. In addition to livestock, the main agricultural crops are sunflower seeds, lemons, soybeans, grapes, corn, tobacco, peanuts, tea, and wheat. The country also benefits from a large tourism industry.

Tourists travel to Argentina to marvel at its natural wonders, including Iguazú Falls.

CHAPTER 9
ARGENTINA TODAY

Argentina has come a long way in the past several decades, transitioning from a brutal military government to a working democracy. The military, reduced in size and power, now plays a much less prominent part in government. Industry has been largely privatized. Even the Catholic Church, which used to have a strong influence on politics, now has a reduced role. In the past, the church was successful in pushing for conservative policies, such as keeping abortion illegal and encouraging intolerance of homosexuals. In recent years, however, the government has broken with the church on some issues, including legalizing same-sex marriage.

While Argentina's constitution guarantees free speech and freedom of the press, journalists still face obstacles. One has been economic: many newspapers have been forced out of business during difficult economic times. This has resulted in fewer voices being represented in the media and a weakened ability to carry out the press's watchdog function.

Freedom of the press has improved in Argentina in recent decades.

enjoy an afternoon nap called a siesta, the busy *porteños* of Buenos Aires have left this tradition behind.

In Buenos Aires, most families live in apartment buildings, while residents of towns and rural areas usually live in small houses. Very large cattle ranches located in the Pampas and other rural areas are called *estancias* and sometimes include their own church and school. Because of the high cost of housing, some Argentine families live with as many as three generations in one home, and the youngest generation does not move out until marriage.

SCHOOLS

Argentina has long placed a high priority on education, resulting in a national literacy rate of 97.2 percent.[5] Education is free and mandatory from ages 6 to 14, but attendance drops after age 14. Students leave school because they have difficulty paying for books and supplies or because they must go to work and help support their families.

The subjects studied include science, math, languages, art, history, sports, and geography. Students recently have gained more freedom to choose what they study in secondary school, which begins in seventh

Argentines usually eat dinner after 9:00 p.m.

Porteños **enjoy the cultural offerings of their cosmopolitan city.**

Eighteen is considered the age of maturity in several respects in Argentina. It is when teens gain the right to vote and the ability to drive legally. Eighteen is also the minimum drinking age. Turning 15 is significant for Argentine girls. On that birthday, girls celebrate their *quinceañera*, which marks the end of childhood.

grade and lasts three or four years. Completing secondary school is required for admission to college. Argentina has public colleges, which are state run and taxpayer funded, and private colleges.

In the past, Argentina was known for its fine education system, but cuts to school funding have become a concern in some places. In 2010, thousands of students marched to the presidential palace to protest the quality of the Buenos Aires schools. Students' complaints included the deterioration of school buildings, some of which lack heat and have leaky ceilings and broken windows.

PAST MEETS FUTURE

The first decade of the twenty-first century offered several opportunities for Argentines to reflect on their history and outlook. In 2006, they marked the 30-year anniversary of the beginning of the Dirty War. Approximately 30,000 Argentines are thought to have lost their lives from 1976 to 1983 as the military systematically tried to eliminate dissent.

Students protest poor school conditions outside the National Congress building in Buenos Aires.

the government remains a concern, and leaders have been known to get around the legislative process by issuing decrees.

Despite these challenges, Argentines are committed to their democracy. In some areas, Argentines have even been world leaders—for instance, in encouraging women to participate in government, in setting strict environmental emissions standards, and in legalizing gay marriage. And most important, Argentines have vowed never again to return to their recent past of human rights abuses, military coups, and state terrorism.

The Argentine people are working toward a more prosperous and democratic future.

KEY PEOPLE

Former president Juan Perón and former First Lady Eva Perón helped the poor while ruling in a dictatorial manner.

Carlos Gardel helped popularize the tango.

Cristina Fernández de Kirchner became the first woman elected president.

PROVINCES OF ARGENTINA

Province; Capital

Buenos Aires; La Plata

Catamarca; Catamarca

Chaco; Resistencia

Chubut; Rawson

Córdoba; Córdoba

Corrientes; Corrientes

Entre Ríos; Paraná

Formosa; Formosa

Jujuy; Jujuy

La Pampa; Santa Rosa

La Rioja; La Rioja

Mendoza; Mendoza

Misiones; Posadas

Neuquén; Neuquén

Río Negro; Viedma

Salta; Salta

San Juan; San Juan

San Luis; San Luis

Santa Cruz; Río Gallegos

Santa Fe; Santa Fe

Santiago del Estero; Santiago del Estero

Tierra del Fuego; Ushuaia

Tucumán; Tucumán

GLOSSARY

anti-Semitism

Hostility toward or discrimination against Jews.

authoritarian

Having power concentrated in the hands of a leader who is not accountable to the people.

biodiversity

The variety of plant and animal life in a particular habitat.

coup

The violent overthrow of an existing government by a small group.

creole

A person of European descent born in Latin America.

default

The failure to pay a financial debt.

ecotourism

The practice of visiting a place in an environmentally friendly way or for the purpose of experiencing its natural features.

federalist

Someone who favors the distribution of power between a central government and smaller political units, such as states and provinces.

gross domestic product

The total value of goods and services in a country, usually measured annually.

guerrilla

Irregular warfare, usually involving sabotage and harassment, that is waged by a small independent group against a stronger military.

inflation

A continuing rise in the general level of prices.

line-item veto

The power of an executive to delete individual words or sentences from a bill without rejecting the entire bill.

mestizos

Mixed-race descendents of Europeans and indigenous peoples.

oligarchy

A government controlled by a small group.

privatize

To change a business or industry from public to private control and ownership.

quota

A fixed share or amount assigned to a group or a member of a group.

recession

A period of reduced economic activity.

subantarctic

Lying just outside the Antarctic Circle.

ADDITIONAL RESOURCES

SELECTED BIBLIOGRAPHY

Baim, Jo. *Tango: Creation of a Cultural Icon*. Bloomington, IN: Indiana UP, 2007. Print.

Black, Jan Knippers, ed. *Latin America: Its Problems and Its Promise*. Cambridge, MA: Westview, 2005. Print.

Brown, Jonathan C. *A Brief History of Argentina*. New York: Facts on File, 2010. Print.

MacLachlan, Colin M. *Argentina: What Went Wrong*. Westport, CT: Praeger, 2006. Print.

Moss, Joyce, and George Wilson. *Peoples of the World: Latin Americans*. Detroit, MI: Gal Research, 1989. Print.

Palmerlee, Danny. *Argentina*. Oakland, CA: Lonely Planet, 2008. Web. 28 Nov. 2010.

FURTHER READINGS

Favor, Lesli J. *Eva Perón*. New York: Benchmark, 2010. Print.

Fearns, Les. *Argentina*. New York: Facts on File, 2005. Print.

Gorrell, Gena K. *In the Land of the Jaguar: South America and Its People*. Toronto, Can.: Tundra, 2007. Print.

Lourie, Peter. *Tierra del Fuego: A Journey to the End of the Earth*. Honesdale, PA: Boyds Mills, 2002. Print.

McCarthy, Rose, and Theodore Link. *Argentina: A Primary Source Cultural Guide*. New York: PowerPlus, 2004. Print.

Whelan, Gloria. *The Disappeared*. New York: Penguin, 2010. Print.

WEB LINKS

To learn more about Argentina, visit ABDO Publishing Company online at **www.abdopublishing.com**. Web sites about Argentina are featured on our Book Links page. These links are routinely monitored and updated to provide the most current information available.

PLACES TO VISIT

If you are ever in Argentina, consider checking out these important and interesting sites!

Casa Rosada and the Presidential Museum

Also known as the Pink Palace, the presidential palace in Buenos Aires offers free, guided tours in Spanish and English on weekends and holidays.

Latin American Art Museum of Buenos Aires

Featuring art and culture from Argentina and Latin America, this museum has been open since 2001.

National Historical Museum

This free museum in Buenos Aires features exhibits on important historical events, such as the May Revolution and Argentine War for Independence.

SOURCE NOTES

CHAPTER 1. A VISIT TO ARGENTINA
1. Wayne Bernhardson. "Buenos Aires: A City of Style—And Sizzle." *National Geographic*. National Geographic Society, Mar. 2010. Web. 11 Dec. 2010.

2. Jan Knippers Black, ed. *Latin America: Its Problems and Its Promise*. Cambridge, MA: Westview, 2005. Print. 541.

3. "The World Factbook: Argentina." *Central Intelligence Agency*. Central Intelligence Agency, 13 Jan. 2011. Web. 31 Jan. 2010.

4. Jan Knippers Black, ed. *Latin America: Its Problems and Its Promise*. Cambridge, MA: Westview, 2005. Print. 541.

5. Danny Palmerlee. *Argentina*. Oakland, CA: Lonely Planet, 2008. Web. 28 Nov. 2010. 17.

CHAPTER 2. GEOGRAPHY: RAIN FORESTS AND GLACIERS
1. "Argentina." *Encyclopædia Britannica*. Encyclopædia Britannica, 2011. Web. 14 Jan. 2011.

2. "The World Factbook: Argentina." *Central Intelligence Agency*. Central Intelligence Agency, 13 Jan. 2011. Web. 31 Jan. 2010.

3. Jonathan C. Brown. *A Brief History of Argentina*. New York: Facts on File, 2010. Print. 304.

4. "Geography." *Embassy of Argentina in Australia*. Embassy of Argentina in Australia, n.d. Web. 8 Jan. 2011.

5. Danny Palmerlee. *Argentina*. Oakland, CA: Lonely Planet, 2008. Web. 28 Nov. 2010. 64.

6. "Country Guide: Argentina." *BBC: Weather*. BBC, n.d. Web. 17 Jan. 2011.

7. "Patagonia Photos: Moreno Glacier." *National Geographic*. National Geographic Society, n.d. Web. 17 Jan. 2011.

8. "The World Factbook: Argentina." *Central Intelligence Agency*. Central Intelligence Agency, 13 Jan. 2011. Web. 31 Jan. 2010.

CHAPTER 3. ANIMALS AND NATURE: FROM PENGUINS TO PUMAS
1. Eric Wagner. "Penguin Dispatch 1: Arriving in Punta Tombo Argentina." *Smithsonian.com*. Smithsonian Institution, 4 June 2009. Web. 9 Jan. 2011.

2. Ibid.

3. Ibid.

4. Danny Palmerlee. *Argentina*. Oakland, CA: Lonely Planet, 2008. Web. 28 Nov. 2010. 78.

5. "Environmental Problems in Argentina." *World Wildlife Fund*. World Wildlife Fund, Web. 9 Jan. 2011.

6. "The IUCN Red List of Threatened Species." *IUCN Red List.* International Union for Conservation of Nature and Natural Resources, 2010. Web. 19 Jan. 2011.

7. "Summary Statistics: Summaries by Country, Table 5, Threatened Species in Each Country." *IUCN Red List of Threatened Species.* International Union for Conservation of Nature and Natural Resources, 2010. Web. 18 Jan. 2011.

8. John Vidal. "Cities in Peril as Andean Glaciers Melt." *Guardian.co.uk.* Guardian News and Media, 29 Aug. 2006. Web. 19 Jan. 2011.

9. Alan Boyle. "Bringing the Biggest Dinosaur to Life." *MSNBC.com.* MSNBC.com, 27 July 2001. Web. 6 Dec. 2010.

10. "Protected Areas." *Argentina.ar.* Media Ministry of the President's Office, 16 Oct. 2007. Web. 31 Jan. 2011.

CHAPTER 4. HISTORY: FROM COLONY TO REPUBLIC

1. Jonathan C. Brown. *A Brief History of Argentina.* New York: Facts on File, 2010. Print. 106.

2. Ibid. 236.

3. Ibid. 238.

4. Jan Knippers Black, ed. *Latin America: Its Problems and Its Promise.* Cambridge, MA: Westview, 2005. Print. 546.

5. Jan Knippers Black, ed. *Latin America: Its Problems and Its Promise.* Cambridge, MA: Westview, 2005. Print. 548.

CHAPTER 5. PEOPLE: A CHANGING NATION

1. Colin M. MacLachlan. *Argentina: What Went Wrong.* Westport, CT: Praeger, 2006. Print. 1.

2. "The World Factbook: Argentina." *Central Intelligence Agency.* Central Intelligence Agency, 13 Jan. 2011. Web. 31 Jan. 2010.

3. Joyce Moss and George Wilson. *Peoples of the World: Latin Americans.* Detroit, MI: Gal Research, 1989. Print. 30.

4. Joyce Moss and George Wilson. *Peoples of the World: Latin Americans.* Detroit, MI: Gal Research, 1989. Print. 32.

5. Jonathan C. Brown. *A Brief History of Argentina.* New York: Facts on File, 2010. Print. 297.

6. "The World Factbook: Argentina." *Central Intelligence Agency.* Central Intelligence Agency, 13 Jan. 2011. Web. 31 Jan. 2010.

SOURCE NOTES CONTINUED

7. "About Argentina/Religion." *Argentina.gov*. Secretaría de Gabinete y Gestión Pública, n.d. Web. 17 Jan. 2011.

8. "The World Factbook: Argentina." *Central Intelligence Agency*. Central Intelligence Agency, 13 Jan. 2011. Web. 31 Jan. 2010.

9. "Background Note: Argentina." *US Department of State*. US Department of State, 16 Sept. 2010. Web. 19 Jan. 2011.

10. Jonathan C. Brown. *A Brief History of Argentina*. New York: Facts on File, 2010. Print. 304.

11. "About Argentina/Major Cities." *Argentina.gov.ar*. Secretaría de Gabinete y Gestión Pública, n.d. Web. 17 Jan. 2011.

CHAPTER 6. CULTURE: THE LAND OF THE TANGO

1. Jo Baim. *Tango: Creation of a Cultural Icon*. Bloomington, IN: Indiana UP, 2007. Print. 3.

2. Jonathan C. Brown. *A Brief History of Argentina*. New York: Facts on File, 2010. Print. 190.

3. Walter Aaron Clark, ed. *From Tejano to Tango: Latin American Popular Music*. New York: Routledge, 2002. Print. 70.

CHAPTER 7. POLITICS: INCREASING STABILITY

1. Jonathan C. Brown. *A Brief History of Argentina*. New York: Facts on File, 2010. Print. 275.

2. Ibid. 278.

3. Ibid. 282.

4. Ibid. 281.

5. "Interview: Cristina Fernandez de Kirchner of Argentina." *TIME*. 29 Sept. 2007. Web. 3 Jan. 2011.

6. "Constitution of the Argentine Nation." *Official Web Site of the Government of Argentina*. Government of Argentina, 1994. Web. 3 Jan. 2011.

7. Ibid.

CHAPTER 8. ECONOMICS: RECOVERING PROSPERITY

1. Colin M. MacLachlan. *Argentina: What Went Wrong*. Westport, CT: Praeger, 2006. Print. viii.

2. Jonathan C. Brown. *A Brief History of Argentina*. New York: Facts on File, 2010. Print. 287.

3. Colin M. MacLachlan. *Argentina: What Went Wrong*. Westport, CT: Praeger, 2006. Print. 120–121.

4. Ibid. 156.

5. Ibid. 169.

6. Danny Palmerlee. *Argentina*. Oakland, CA: Lonely Planet, 2008. Web. 28 Nov. 2010. 39.

7. Mark Weisbrot. "Nestor Kirchner: Argentina's Independence Hero." *Guardian.co.uk*. Guardian News and Media, 27 Oct. 2010. Web. 16 Jan. 2011.

8. "The World Factbook: Argentina." *Central Intelligence Agency*. Central Intelligence Agency, 13 Jan. 2011. Web. 31 Jan. 2010.

9. Ibid.

10. Mark P. Sullivan. "Argentina: Political and Economic Conditions and U.S. Relations." *CRS Report for Congress*. Congressional Research Service, 12 Oct. 2006. Web. 16 Jan. 2011.

11. Jonathan C. Brown, *A Brief History of Argentina*. New York: Facts on File, 2010. Print. 304.

12. "The World Factbook: Argentina." *Central Intelligence Agency*. Central Intelligence Agency, 13 Jan. 2011. Web. 31 Jan. 2010.

13. Ibid.

14. "The World Factbook: Argentina." *Central Intelligence Agency*. Central Intelligence Agency, 13 Jan. 2011. Web. 31 Jan. 2010.

15. Ibid.

CHAPTER 9. ARGENTINA TODAY

1. Colin M. MacLachlan. *Argentina: What Went Wrong*. Westport, CT: Praeger, 2006. Print. 167.

2. Alexei Barrionuevo. "Argentina Approves Gay Marriage, in a First for Region." *New York Times*. New York Times, 15 July 2010. Web. 17 Jan. 2011.

3. "Lifestyle." *Estudiar en Argentina*. Ministerio de Educación, Argentina, 2011. Web. 17 Jan. 2011.

4. Olivia Keetch. "Smoking in Argentina: Youth Targeted?" *Argentina Independent*. Argentina Independent, 22 Feb. 2008. Web. 17 Jan. 2011.

5. "The World Factbook: Argentina." *Central Intelligence Agency*. Central Intelligence Agency, 13 Jan. 2011. Web. 31 Jan. 2010.

6. Larry Rohter. "Recalling Coup, Argentina Vows 'Never Again.'" *New York Times*. New York Times, 26 Mar. 2006. Web. 17 Jan. 2011.

INDEX

INDEX CONTINUED

PHOTO CREDITS

iStockphoto, cover, 69, 115, 116; Eduardo Rivero/Shutterstock Images, 2, 9, 44, 97, 131; Pablo Hernan/Fotolia, 5 (top), 120; Wojciech Zwierzynski/iStockphoto, 5 (middle), 29; Nicolas Larento/Fotolia, 5 (bottom), 36; Cristian Lazzari/iStockphoto, 6, 133; Gary Yim/Shutterstock Images, 11, 94; Dan Cooper/iStockphoto, 13; Daniel Korzeniewski/Shutterstock Images, 15; Matt Kania/Map Hero, Inc., 16, 23, 31, 71, 113; Manda Nicholls/Shutterstock Images, 20; Irina Bazhanova/iStockphoto, 25; Klaus-Peter Wolf/Photolibrary, 32; J-L. Klein & M-L. Hubert/ Photolibrary, 35; Galina Barskaya/Shutterstock Images, 39, 130; Mike Theiss/Getty Images, 42; London Stereoscopic Company/Getty Images, 47; Anibal Trejo/Fotolia, 49, 128 (top); AP Images, 52, 128 (bottom); Eduardo Di Baia/AP Images, 57, 59, 129 (top); Raul Ferrari/AP Images, 60; Shutterstock Images, 62, 108, 126; The Print Collector/Photolibrary, 65; Diego Alvarez de Toledo/iStockphoto, 73; Juan Mabromata/AFP/Getty Images, 74; Jacek Kadaj/ Shutterstock Images, 79; Kevork Djansezian/Getty Images, 81; Daniel Korzeniewski/iStockphoto, 84; Katarzyna Citko/Shutterstock Images, 86; Andrea Priotti/Fotolia, 88, 132; Daniel Luna/AP Images, 91, 129 (bottom); Colman Lerner Gerardo/Shutterstock Images, 99; Federico Igea/ Fotolia, 102; John Phillips/Time & Life Pictures/Getty Images, 105; Mark Edwards/Photolibrary, 111; Natacha Pisarenko/AP Images, 123